THE INCIVILITY SOLUTION:

TOOLS TO FOSTER SELF-TRANSCENDENCE FOR NURSE EDUCATORS

Cynthia Keeton Brown

BALBOA.
PRESS
A DIVISION OF HAY HOUSE

Balboa Press books may be ordered through booksellers or by contacting:

Balboa Press
A Division of Hay House
1663 Liberty Drive
Bloomington, IN 47403
www.balboapress.com
1 (877) 407-4847

Because of the dynamic nature of the Internet, any web addresses or links contained in this book may have changed since publication and may no longer be valid. The views expressed in this work are solely those of the author and do not necessarily reflect the views of the publisher, and the publisher hereby disclaims any responsibility for them.

The author of this book does not dispense medical advice or prescribe the use of any technique as a form of treatment for physical, emotional, or medical problems without the advice of a physician, either directly or indirectly. The intent of the author is only to offer information of a general nature to help you in your quest for emotional and spiritual well-being. In the event you use any of the information in this book for yourself, which is your constitutional right, the author and the publisher assume no responsibility for your actions.

Any people depicted in stock imagery provided by Thinkstock are models, and such images are being used for illustrative purposes only.
Certain stock imagery © Thinkstock.

Print information available on the last page.

ISBN: 978-1-5043-5708-1 (sc)
ISBN: 978-1-5043-5709-8 (e)

Balboa Press rev. date: 09/02/2016

For nurses everywhere, my gift to you.

ABSTRACT

The significance of the problem of incivility in nursing education is well researched and documented in nursing scholarly literature (Clark, 2013). The evidence suggests that nursing faculty is positioned at the front line in terms of turning back the impending tide of incivility in nursing education (Clark, 2013). One individual at a time, starting with ourselves; nurse educators have the ability to promulgate a culture of civility among colleagues, with students in the classroom, at clinical partner sites and in the community. This project suggests that nurse educators who cultivate mindfulness, knowing, authentic learning and engage students with dignity and respect can curb if not stop incivility from creeping into the learning environment. A literature review was conducted using Cochrane, PubMed, EBSCO, CINAHL, Medline and Ovid to familiarize the author with the concept of incivility in nursing education, nursing theory and teaching learning strategies to determine where and how this problem in nursing practice can be effectively solved and the implications for nursing education going forward. Key terms included: incivility, bullying, nursing education, self-transcendence, humanism, behaviorism, caring theory and holistic taxonomy, active learning and assessment.

ACKNOWLEDGMENTS

I would like to express my deepest gratitude to Dr. Heather Fenton, Dr. Jodi Gooden and Dr. Diana Mashburn. My nursing education at Northeastern State University has been one of the biggest joys of my life. The past five years has been so full and rich. Thank you for your constant support, input and encouragement. Without it, this project may not have come to completion.

I would also like to thank the many authors of spiritual teachings that are referenced in this project for their amazing work. These are all wonderful people with beautiful lessons to impart regarding the enormity of human potential and that influence kindness, goodness and compassion in the world.

Vicki Karlovich, thank you so much for giving me my first crack at a leadership position. Your enthusiasm and trust encourage me every day.

Finally, I would like to thank my daughter Lily and especially my late husband T. Logan Brown for their ongoing and unwavering support. Without them my Master of Science in Nursing Education would not have been possible. They were there cheering me up and pushing me forward. T. Logan Brown always supported and encouraged me with his best wishes, loving input and constant praise.

TABLE OF CONTENTS

SECTION I

INTRODUCTION

Nurse researchers have been studying incivility in nursing education for more than a few decades. We have all experienced some form of incivility in our nursing practice. Incivility can occur in a variety of a myriad of forms from eye rolling to physical violence (Clark, 2013). Incivility has been defined many times over and can be described as a toxic environment where interactions between people are uncivil, rude, unsociable, ungracious, impolite, disrespectful, cruel, or even violent. Bullying has become a more common buzzword; however bullying and incivility differ (Roberts, 2015). Bullying consists of victimization whereas incivility is found at times to be a lateral form of violence. Incivility in nurse education can be faculty to faculty, student to faculty, faculty to student, student to student. These would be examples of lateral incivility in the workplace or in institutions of higher learning.

This author suggests that nurse educators who understand incivility and co-create an environment of civility in their respective workplaces can positively impact their lives and those of their colleagues and students. Tools to foster self-transcendence in nurse educators are presented to teach the teacher to use multiple intelligences; emotional intelligence, knowing and authentic learning experiences to guide a daily practice of forgiveness, empathy and gratitude. The teachings of prominent contemporary spiritual teachers are utilized to promote civil behavior in individuals as a daily choice. The daily practice that is suggested pertains to how the nurse educator participates in self-care and focuses on mindful awareness during interactions with colleagues, students and community. Role-modeling the desired behavior of civility by nurse educators is the first step to confronting the problem of incivility in nursing education. The expectation or returns will show up as less stressful days, improved learning outcomes for students, decreased student attrition and reduced faculty turnover.

This guidebook will include a needs assessment, literature review, teaching learning plan and evaluation method for the proposed project. Ultimately resulting in a multimedia seminar consisting of learning modules that describe and define what incivility is, why it happens, what we as nurse educators can do about it right now. Also included is the design of an evaluation tool that will collect qualitative and quantitative data on the nurse educator's perceptions of incivility and the effectiveness of the seminar for a future research project and quality improvement initiatives.

Problem Statement

Incivility in the workplace in nursing education is a problem. This author has experienced and or witnessed disrespectful behavior from classmates, co-workers and administration in virtually every healthcare setting including long term care, hospital, home health, and in institutions of higher learning. Who has not had a physician be a total jerk to them on the floor? Who has not been ignored or discouraged during a clinical rotation when a seasoned nurse has not wanted to be shadowed? Who has not witnessed a co-worker crying in the break room after an unpleasant exchange with a patient or co-worker?

Bullying is the terminology most used in the media right now, rather than incivility. When a work or school environment becomes toxic staff turnover and student withdrawals are bound to be higher and job satisfaction lower. In a recent national study, 68% of nursing faculty reported moderate to serious levels of faculty-to-faculty incivility in their nursing programs (Clark, Olender, Kenski, & Cardoni, 2013). Low morale, increased illness, isolation and alienation have purported to lead to increased absenteeism, work decline and many nursing faculty leave their positions to seek a climate that is tenable (Clark, 2013).

In the case of the Oikos Christian University: School of Nursing shooting in Oakland in 2012; a former student targeted the school of nursing and a particular administrator. Seven were left dead after the rampage. This was the worst school shooting in U.S. history since the Virginia Tech shooting in 2007 (Park & Jones, 2012). The police reported that One Goh was so upset about being teased about his poor English skills that he had been planning the attack for weeks. It was not reported as to whether or not Goh was dismissed from the program or if he left voluntarily (Park & Jones, 2012). This is an example of the worst kind of violence that incivility can lead to; when people are dressed down systematically and are subjected to psychological abuse the violence can proceed to physical retaliation.

Purpose of the Project

The purpose of this project is to sustain nursing education faculty with the tools to recognize uncivil behavior and the risks and outcomes associated with it while outlining behaviors that build on civility, compassion, courage and empathy. These qualities foster self-transcendence and can effectively combat incivility in nursing education. Beginning with ourselves and taking self-responsibility for the kinds of behavior that we exhibit to each other as faculty, to our students and the community we can begin to see a change and nurse educators can begin to co-create a culture of civility in nursing education that can spread beyond our classrooms, higher learning institutions and into our health systems, and will concurrently positively impact our interactions with our families.

Conceptual Framework

The nursing theory utilized for the framework of this project is Watson's Caring Science Theory. Watson describes Caritas nursing as a caring that is aware of other and that the Caring Science is one that the ethical dimension precludes the technical and biomedical paradigms (2008). Watson is particularly cognizant of the need for nursing education to reintroduce humanism; love and emotions and to see the face behind the case (Watson, 2008).

Hauenstein's Holistic Taxonomy is selected because it is a particularly meaningful taxonomy due to the inclusion of the behavior domain. Candela explains the behavior domain as, "the tempered demeanor that one displays as a reaction to social stimulus, or an inner need, or both" (Keating, p.78). Outcomes are selected based on not only cognitive, affective and psychomotor skills but the behavior and new skills adaptation by nurse faculty going forward; past knowing.

Maslow's Theory of Self-Transcendence is the backdrop for the development of the significance and potential solutions for the problem of incivility in nursing education. Maslow describes transcendence as the next possible step after self-actualization that is driven by wisdom particularly later in life. The behaviors associated with self-transcendence include moving beyond shortcomings, finding courage, and demonstrating independence which includes a certain disregard for old modes of doing things in favor of achieving sense of self, connection with others and higher awareness despite the social convictions that may be pervasive in certain contexts. In particular, achieving a unity with the next generation was pointed out as especially linked to greater meaningfulness (McCarthey & Bockweg, 2013). These three primary theories form the conceptual framework for the proposed project.

Operational Definitions

Empathy is the verbal or non-verbal demonstration of understanding and acceptance and can be a skill or trait that leads to a potential uplifting and healing exchange between individuals (Brown, 2014).

Holistic Nursing requires nurses to integrate self-care, self-responsibility, spirituality, and reflection in their lives; which may lead the nurse to greater awareness of the interconnectedness with self, others, nature, and spirit (AHNA, 2015).

Mindful Awareness may further enhance the nurses understanding of all individuals and their relationships to the human and global community, and permits nurses to use this awareness to facilitate the healing process (AHNA, 2915).

Self-Transcendence is Maslow's way of describing a late life developmental process that has a profound affect within the spiritual domain (McCarthy & Bockweg, 2013).

Significance

According to Clark (2013), "skilled leaders are needed to boldly address the insidious nature and related consequences of faculty-to-faculty incivility to improve the moral and ethical fabric of the academic culture," (p. 102). This project goes to the very beginning, we as faculty exhibit the behaviors that our students pick up on and mirror. Faculty must take responsibility to treat each other with mutual respect and refuse to fall into uncivil behavior. Faculty can set the bar high and use thoughtful techniques, gentle strategies and loving concepts to cure and heal ourselves, our interrelationships, our departments and our institutions. This project will provide faculty nurse educators with tools to foster self-transcendence that will provide an incivility solution for academic settings in nursing education that is desperately needed and wanted. In Clark's 2013 study respondents called for leadership and described leaders as those who are honest, effective, and competent and are positive role models and can exist at multiple levels of the organization. In addition, demonstration of the damage that incongruous behavior by faculty can proliferate when incivility goes unchecked in the nursing education setting is explored.

SECTION II

LITERATURE REVIEW

Several important studies have looked deeply into the topic of incivility in nursing education. Roberts (2015) review documents lateral violence and how the terminology and efforts to discourage incivility in nursing have evolved over the last three decades. Roberts calls out oppressed group theory whereby members of the group can develop disdain for their group members because of long held internal beliefs of their own inferiority. These negative belief systems create a cycle of fear, anxiety and the inability to form a sense of unity necessary to support each other effectively to gain power (Roberts, 2015). Roberts also found in her research that teaching nurses about marginalization, the dynamics of oppression and that uncivil behavior is intolerable could be helpful in dealing positively with staff or faculty behaviors. Roberts work suggests that the relationship of leadership and power in the workplace requires further study. Uncivil behavior is not limited to demeaning behaviors and passive aggressive communication plays a significant role in inter-group competition (Roberts, 2015).

This problem was studied with a sample of nurse educators by Clark (2013) and several behaviors were identified using the Faculty to Faculty Incivility Survey (F-FI Survey). Behaviors most mentioned in the qualitative findings from the study include in descending order were: Berating, insulting and allowing; setting up, undermining, and sabotaging; power playing, derailing, and disgracing; excluding, gossiping, degrading; refusing, not doing, and justifying; blaming and accusing; taking credit (ripping off) the work of others; distracting and disrupting, during meetings. Clark points out that limitation of the study includes the inability to baseline the perceptions as each participant has an individual interpretation of the severity of the behaviors reported. Included in Clark's discussion were the participants' requests for faculty workshops, skill development to increase knowledge on how to communicate effectively, and the use of civility consultants to help faculty engage in meaningful discussions surrounding incivility in nursing education and solution finding (Clark, 2015).

Altmiller's focus group exploratory study used concept analysis for data collection to call out student's perceptions of what faculty incivility looks like. Themes and subthemes were identified. The top five themes called out by Altmiller are: unprofessional behavior, poor communication techniques, power gradient, inequality and loss of control over one's world. The study demonstrated that students and faculty see uncivil behavior much the same (Altmiller, 2015). Insight's from Altmiller's study includes that civil and or uncivil behavior is learned and reinforced through repetition. The perception that student and faculty incivility is justified one by the other creates a dangerous learning environment. One of the solutions presented is that boundaries between student and faculty should not be blurred and that faculty must always practice and maintain civil behavior and appropriate response particularly when faced with negative or violent behavior from students (Altmiller, 2015).

The purpose of Robertson's (2012) study was for the author to obtain a broadened understanding of factors that are increasing the incidence of incivility in nursing education. Robertson uses several research definitions of incivility and contemplates that the unifying component of all the definitions is that the learning process is halted when it takes place (Robertson, 2012). Consequently, when faculty are preoccupied with disciplining students and students are under disciplinary action it takes away from the learning of the art and science of nursing and is a major detractor for the entire learning environment (Roberson, 2012). Additionally, students can go into the workplace unprepared to be professional nurses when uncivil behavior is not addressed or goes unrecognized. Importantly student factors that may profile the uncivil student include maladaptation to the high stress environment of nursing school, which can include academic, financial and other stressors such as role adjustment. High levels of frustration, depression and fear can result in anger and the uncivil behavior (Robertson, 2015).

Luparell's (2011), commentary bridges a gap regarding incivility in nursing by identifying a connection between academia and clinical settings in so much as that nursing students are going to be our colleagues in the nursing profession. In the clinical setting we ask nurses to precept our students, if our student nurses are treated badly by their clinical counterparts and their faculty repeatedly; would it not be a natural presupposition that nursing students would portend to exemplify the same behavior demonstrated by their mentors (Luparell, 2011). Luparell further points out that critical examination of how students are socialized into the nursing profession, in clinical and academic settings is important. Preceptors and faculty who are empowered and able to communicate to students, colleagues and other faculty about and with the less tangible skills related to appropriate communication can foster therapeutic relationships when performing critiques, suggestions, assessments or evaluations (Luparell, 2011).

Anthony & Yastik's (2011) examination of nursing student's experience showed similar trends in the clinical setting. The themes that emerged from this qualitative study included three areas of perceived incivility: exclusionary (we're in the way), hostile or rude (we were always in tears), and dismissive (they just walk away) (Anthony & Yastik, 2011). When students were asked what experiences in the clinical setting were positive for you? The students most often reported; being included in patient care activities. Demonstrating the inclusionary aspect of being approached by staff nurses to assist with direct patient care was particularly valued. Interesting on the third question students were asked what they thought that nursing faculty should do about incivility in the clinical setting? The student nurses most commonly thought that nothing could be done about the situation. However, they did agree when they became professional nurses they would bring about change by including and valuing nursing students (Anthony & Yastik, 2011).

A survey conducted on incivility in the workplace for new graduate nurses; the effects on their mental health and the cultivation of resiliency to combat the negative effects of incivility were studied by Laschinger, Wong & Regan (2013). Their literature review discussed coworker, supervisor and physician incivility being apparent across studies and although measured at varying degrees the statistics were very disheartening in the face of the nursing shortage (AACN, 2014). Incivility in the workplace increases staff turnover. Their findings suggest that workplace incivility from anyone in the workplace can have negative effects on the new nurses' mental health and that resiliency can provide a protective factor from co-worker incivility that tends to have a particularly damaging effect. Laschinger et al. (2013) also suggest that nursing management should do everything possible to create respectful supportive work environments that assist new graduates to transition from novice to expert.

Hawkins (2015) review reveals that the concepts of respect and disrespect reflect a rhythmical pattern and is often a perception denoted by communication. The way we communicate with people denotes to them whether or not we respect or disrespect them. Demonstrating value rather than conveying derogatory remarks communicates respect. Oppositely, disrespect was found in the literature to mostly coincide with the recipients feelings of anger, shame and uncertainty. Hawkins ascertains that our day to day encounters with individuals, groups an even nations can impact quality of living and she points to Leininger's Theory of Human Becoming as a significant aspect to the expressions and patterns of how we treat people as being a sign of reverence for another, accepting of their inherent worth which relates to seeing humanity in others and acting accordingly to lessen suffering.

McCarthy & Bockweg (2013) look at self-transcendence as component or concept of successful aging from a holistic viewpoint. Maslow's Theory of Self-Transcendence is reviewed in great detail and linked back to the original theory of self-actualization. Examples are laid out in relation to generativity, connectedness and meaning in life.

McCarthy & Bockweg (2013) point out that:

> Maslow's definition is extrapolated as the form of the verb transcend and the meaning is to rise above or move beyond time, culture, self, and others. Maslow identified other self-transcendence behaviors as moving beyond weakness, fears, and dependency; transcending the opinions or expectations of others, such as social conventions, family roles, or a focus on others to the exclusion of self: achieving a since of unity with oneself, others – especially the next generation – and

a higher power; and possessing an awareness of a greater meaning
in life. (p. 86)

Clark, Nguyen & Barbosa-Leiker conducted a three year longitudinal study using descriptive, repeated-measures, survey design to describe nursing students perceptions of coping with stress and faculty student and faculty relationships. The research lays out potential strategies to promote civility in nursing education. The students described that communication, flexibility and encouragement from faculty could reduce stress and provide increased coping abilities. These students also discussed activities that promoted stress reduction included talking with family and friends and spending time outdoors reduced their stress surrounding their academic pursuits. Lastly, Clark et al. discusses the importance of co-creating an environment of respect where lively discussion can still thrive; a safe classroom is where differences of opinion are respected and encouraged (Clark, Nguyen & Barbosa-Leiker, 2014).

SECTION III

THE PROJECT

This project is designed to give nurse educators tools to foster their own self-transcendence in the area of civility in nursing education. When the nurse educator takes self-responsibility for their own beliefs, attitudes, mannerisms and communication skills and attributes; the nurse educator can more effectively mentor students and colleagues.

Selection and Rationale

Incivility in nursing education has been well documented (Clark, 2013), and furthermore incivility has no place in nursing education. Our society in general has grown to be more hostile in institutions of higher learning (Walker, van Jaarsveld & Skarlicki, 2011). The advent of social media has made it very easy for people to bully, make rude comments and essentially harass people anonymously in the past decade.

This project is meaningful in that it is the next logical step to address incivility in nursing education. Given the previous exploratory research there is much to be done to find ways to decrease incivility in nursing education; this is the first place to start on the level of the individual, self-responsibility coupled with meaningful communication and a conscious decision to be giving in our interactions with others.

Context

Faculty who are rigid, devoid of caring, that reach out to students without respect and demonstrate the adherence to oppressive pedagogies are where the tug of war begins (Robertson, 2012). Students are faced with an unending barrage of responsibilities to juggle and can often times be unprepared for the realities of nursing school. This leads to increased stress and anxiety that for some may become unmanageable (Davis,2013).

The seminar developed here focuses on faculty taking self-responsibility for learning new ways and revisiting old ways of doing things that are self-nurturing. When faculty conduct themselves in a manner that conveys patience, caring, genuine concern, and when that genuine concern can be communicated in a sincere way that is not judgmental, cruel or dismissive the student and faculty have an opportunity to potentially elevate complex and difficult situations that can arise during the course of a nursing school program.

Students are listening, watching; when they experience successful interactions they will mirror those behaviors and attitudes that they find to be pleasant. When students are shown a kindness especially when the specifics surrounding a particular interaction have the potential to be negative it can have the biggest impact. If faculty are willing to be the mentors that students really need and respect; we will see a reciprocal relationship in return.

This seminar will provide tools, knowledge and suggestions on ways of being that honor the individual and other (Watson, 2008). When faculty practices empathy, patience, kindness and self-control; potentially any negative or uncivil exchange can be avoided, diffused or resolved. Often times we have to learn to treat ourselves with the same loving kindness first to truly be able to demonstrate and offer it to others.

People are naturally going to cooperate more fully when their feelings are considered and when they feel safe. A conscious decision to use non-threatening, supportive communication at all times and particularly in times of high stress, intense responsibility and also when differences of opinion need to be explored civilly is the place to start (Clark, 2013). This seminar suggests a daily practice for nursing faculty to learn how to return to civility in the face of incivility through the use of mindful awareness and other techniques.

Partnerships

Other partnerships could be fostered with local nursing schools to help build community capacity. Providing the modules to faculty and students would increase awareness of what incivility is and to teach the best methods of reducing incidents of uncivil behavior. The seminar being adapted for use in a clinical setting would be a wonderful opportunity to share the learning with our hospital systems that may improve the quality of mentorship opportunities that already exist.

Objectives

By the end of the seminar nursing faculty will:

1. Recognize incivility in nursing education.
2. Realize that self-responsibility for civil behavior is the best defense to incivility in nursing education.
3. Recognize mind-body interactions and disease, effects of stress and psychophysiological response of the body to incivility, PTSD and potential for violence.
4. Discuss resiliency and the role resiliency plays in decreasing stress, anxiety, insecurity.
5. Apply mindful awareness, patience, and empathy to a daily practice of promoting civility in nursing education.
6. Demonstrate appropriate responses to stressful situations to diffuse potentially uncivil exchanges.
7. Distinguish best practices, intrapersonal relationships; inventory appropriate behaviors that promote civility in nursing education.
8. Plan self-nurturance practices, self-care practices to combat fatigue, job burnout and promote patience and increase job satisfaction.
9. Value the nursing profession, learning through adversity, celebrate accomplishments.
10. Select positive attributes to emphasize, negative behaviors to stop, implementation of these attributes and behaviors.
11. Prepare to engage students, colleagues, clinical sites and community.

12. Appraise and choose classroom tools such as the No Tolerance Incivility Policy and Pledge (see Appendix A for sample).

Components

This seven module seminar (see Appendix B for curriculum outline) takes an in depth look at incivility and what nursing educators can do right now to reduce negative thoughts, behaviors and interactions with students that are not conducive to a civil environment. Contemporary spiritual teachers are cited through the use of readings, video and audio to explore contemplative thought surrounding the concepts of empathy, caring, gratitude, kindness and the cultivation of resilience and the potential for positive impact of appropriate response.

The humanities are utilized to support methodologies and teaching, including music, myth and art. Nursing faculty are encourage to explore new ways of coping with stress, including self-reflection, meditation and cultivating a deeper understanding of the concepts of empathy, courage, compassion, love and forgiveness. Associations are made from conception of ideas to practical uses of strategies in the workplace to increase the quality of collaborative interactions. Lastly, the latest research on incivility, impact on patient safety and other classroom tools are provided as touch points for nurse educators to take to their respective departments and institutions to promote civility within their student's, coworkers, patients and communities.

SECTION IV

IMPLEMENTATION CONSIDERATIONS

This seminar is in line with the Institute of Medicine's (IOM) call for research into "how effective collaboration among groups of health care practitioners with differing characteristics—such as different skill levels (novice nurses versus competent, proficient, or expert nurses) and different duration of employment (e.g., rotating residents and float nurses)—be achieved? What other factors influence effective collaboration, and what strategies are effective in addressing them? It is this author's belief that appropriate civil communication is the foundation from which collaborative groups and teams can be successful. The Institute of Medicine is also asking for other questions to be answered that this seminar can begin to address such as: How do environmental influences affect team performance? For example, what are the effects of stress, organizational culture, and leadership in facilitating or structuring collaborative care? (IOM, 2004).

Additionally, evidence suggests that a broader focus on interpersonal interactions and dynamics within teams can contribute to favorable outcomes (IOM, 2004). Researchers also stress the multiple ways in which health care workers interact in dyads, small groups, and unit-based teams, focusing on the characteristics of the interpersonal behaviors that facilitate effective interaction, decision making, and error-prevention performance may be more useful than a restricted focus on team behavior (IOM, 2004). The IOM committee report (see additional comments Appendix A) on research and collaborative care concludes that there is a need to better understand the mechanisms that produce effective collaboration and team processes can be reviewed with links to research.

Other implementation considerations include size of seminar group, potential implications depending on location of implementation site. Implementation site must have adequate technology including computers with internet access and presentation equipment necessary for display of learning modules in PowerPoint format. Embedded video utilized and sound required for quality display of all materials. The material could be adapted to an online format to be available for individual participation or continuing education unit (CEU) format. The

PowerPoints would be implemented to share in an online format and the needs assessment and post experience surveys could be completed online.

The quality of the presentation materials will be important to the participants' receptiveness to the seminar. Graphics, video and sound need to be of good quality and visually appealing. The materials reviewed and collected for the modules includes the work of many authors that may require special permissions before being utilized in any use beyond this proposal. If special permission is not obtained sections of the seminar may need to be deleted and reworked prior to the modules being presented.

Instructional Strategy - Didactic Questioning - Direct Instruction

Didactic or Oral questioning in standard lecture onsite classrooms can be very helpful for review of student knowledge and assessment of student knowledge. These types of questions allow the student to demonstrate knowledge (Avant & Walker, 2012). The instructor asks the students open ended questions.

In an Onsite/Online Hybrid course the student is offered online tutorials in addition to traditional lecture. This type of questioning can be used in either a low tech or hi tech mode. Faculty can develop a question set rather quickly and does not require any special equipment. Montenery, et al., in 2013, discovered that immediate feedback is also possible, which was "shown to be a millennial preference for their learning experience whether classroom or online based" (p. 377).

According to Gagnon, Gagnon, Desmartis, & Njoya (2013), their research, the teaching method was found to have no direct impact on knowledge acquisition, but the blended classroom was more motivating for some students. When adding the didactic questioning in the classroom to review the online tutorials completed outside of the classroom, it can be a motivator for the student to want to be able to verbally respond in a manner consistent with the learning obtained outside of the classroom. This could be seen as a disadvantage if the technique is viewed by the student as threatening (Avant & Walker, 2012).

- Define Holistic Nursing.
- Explain the meaning of Empathy in Nursing Caring Science

This technique allows for assessment of all ranges of cognitive domain; affective, formative and summative (Avant & Walker, 2012). The instructor asks the students open ended questions and provides immediate feedback as part of evaluation and assessment of student learning. The criteria for assessment should be provided to the students ahead of time and should be fully developed before the session begins (Avant & Walker, 2012).

Instructional Strategy - Cooperative Learning - Interactive Instruction

Koestler & Konopasek (2013) discuss that small group teaching is defined by group size, usually 6 to 10 participants, and a focus on active learning and communication between members of the group. Sessions can occur in a conference room, an administrative or clinical office, or even at the bedside of a patient. You will need to assure that the room is large enough for everyone to be able to sit and make eye contact. Tutorials, seminars, and attending rounds are the traditional modes of small group instruction. Small groups can be effective in accomplishing many tasks:

- Introduction of new material/concepts (self-awareness and self-transcendence)
- Review of material
- Application of material through active learning
- Journal club discussion of video's, scenarios, etc.
- Scenario formats for review, introduction, integration, or application of material
- Student and Colleague-centered discussions
- Team projects

This method also provides an opportunity for integration of domains such as professionalism, humanism, communication skills, and self-directed learning into the formal instruction of the curriculum.

This technique is similar to the focused, scenario discussions, but encourages increased learner independence. Problem based learning (PBL) can be part of a small group (ideally 4-6 members), Students are first presented with a clinical problem such as incivility in nursing education for example. Students define the facts, develop hypotheses based on these facts, and then develop their own learning objectives and plan for solving the clinical problem. At the beginning of each session, students' self-assign their roles in the session, as Leader (moderator), Reader, Scribe, or Participant. These roles will rotate with subsequent sessions, ensuring maximum active participation from all members in the group. Learning objectives are researched between sessions by students and presented back to the group for discussion. This type of small group fosters self-directed learning and teamwork among participants. The faculty member's role in PBL is to facilitate this process, rather than to direct and lead it.

Students also learn to work more independently, and there is a greater focus on self-directed learning. Teamwork is encouraged. PBL takes more in-class time than other methods and faculty have less control over the learning environment than in focused discussions because they function as facilitators of the process and not discussion leaders. Allowing students to struggle with a problem is an important part of the small group learning process. An effective facilitator will accomplish the following tasks:

- Prepare, or assign preparation of, material to be used
- Negotiate and check agreement on small group learning objectives and ground rules
- Facilitate small group activities and discussion
- Provide focus as needed
- Check that learning objectives are attained and tasks are completed
- Troubleshoot problems in group dynamics

- Monitor the flow of the session and attend to time management
- Assess and give feedback on student performance

In small group teaching, the faculty member should view himself as a facilitator of discussion rather than as an instructor. The facilitator's primary function is to structure an effective small group learning environment.

The homework lesson is small group problem based learning that is completed online on a discussion board or via email, skype or whatever method the group has access to. The group divides the homework into equal parts and each participant completes their part. The group arrives at the classroom for the next session with the print out of the completed homework to discuss or critique, feedback is provided by the group and faculty. The group refines their discussion before the next session to add any new learning's, increased knowledge and refinement based on feedback. The instructor facilitates the deepening discussion.

Instructional Strategy - Role Play - Experiential Learning

The definition of role play in nursing education according to Rowles is: "a dramatic approach in which individuals assume the roles of others; usually unscripted, spontaneous interactions (may be semi-structured) that is observed by others for analysis and interpretation" (p.275).

Nursing students using role play in the classroom works best generally in small groups (Rowels, 2012). There are three stages of role playing including briefing, running and debriefing. Briefing includes setting the story to be acted out, setting the stage and an explanation of objectives to be met. Running is the active dramatic portion or the role play; generally can take 5-20 minutes. Debriefing includes discussion, evaluation and reflection or analysis of the outcomes of the role play. Students can describe their experiences and reactions to the role play. The debriefing should take approximately 45 minutes for meaningful discussion.

Role play can increase the nursing students observational skill set while at the same time affecting decision making skills positively (Rowels, 2012). Role play also can increase comprehension and understanding of complex human behaviors. It is important for the faculty leading the sessions to hold criticism to the behaviors exhibited during the role play not to specific students themselves (Rowels, 2012). These types of role play are considered conversational and generally will not use props, scenery or a script for that matter and can be typically incorporated into curriculum without increasing cost. Role playing a disaster plan could be particularly helpful (see Appendix D for commentary on importance of a disaster plan).

SECTION V

EVALUATION OF PROJECT

The evaluation tool will include a survey and a journaling aspect to collect information for quality improvement of the seminar material. Participants will have the opportunity to provide input and discussion in the form of journaling and survey completion. Evaluation of the curriculum can also be gleaned during a question and answer period at the completion of the curriculum during the seminar.

Outcome Measures

Outcome measures would be base lined pre-seminar (see Appendix E for Needs Assessment) based on participant's perceptions. Information could be collected post seminar and then 3 to 6 months out post seminar to evaluate the efficacy of the seminar in promoting civility in nursing education over time (see Appendix F for Post-Seminar Survey). The seminar has a daily practice component and the seminar is not the final learning outcome and should have a long term positive effect on the participant. Outcome measures are not limited to but should include the following:

1. Effect on perceived collegiality.
2. Effect on perceived interactions:
    a. Faculty to Faculty
    b. Student to Faculty
    c. Faculty to Student
    d. Student to Student
3. Effect on perceived job satisfaction, job burnout, compassion fatigue.
4. Effect on overall stress levels, workplace, clinical setting, home life.
5. Effect on Faculty Turnover.
6. Effect on Student Attrition.
7. Effect on Patient Safety.

Effect is intended to measure either an increase, decrease or no change.

Reflections

Clark's (2013) participants request for faculty workshops, and skill development to increase knowledge on how to communicate effectively, and the use of civility consultants to help faculty engage in meaningful discussions surrounding incivility in nursing education and solution finding; lends support. The general interest, nursing faculty are expressing is the need to address the issues of incivility; and point to the taking of self-responsibility that the seminar design is framed around. The seminar proposed here is offered at a time that the audience is ready to hear the message of civility and to solve the problem of incivility in nursing education. This project is meaningful in that the discipline of nursing education should exemplar professional behavior, provide mentorship and support collaborative relationships (IOM, 2004).

Altmiller's work found that civil and or uncivil behavior is learned and reinforced through repetition. The predicted outcomes from the availability of the seminar utilized by faculty would be to practice civility, on-going in daily workplace settings. The seminar is not a once and done training, it is teaching a way of being, knowing and constantly reframing interactions, exchanges and collaborative efforts to increase respect, communication, collaboration and ultimately to reinforce civil behavior through repetition and the daily practice.

Walker et al. (2011) points to the importance of building employees' skills to address incivility within the encounter, as opposed to strategies designed to fix the relationship once the employee has reacted uncivilly toward the customer. Nurses and nurse faculty can cultivate a skill set to learn to appropriately deal with incivility in the moment that it is happening. The seminar guides thinking, uses practical strategies and coping mechanisms to motivate the nursing faculty to always think first before speaking and to be calm when incivility raises its ugly head. The ability to focus, practice mindful awareness and to stay steady during situations that are emotionally charged is the way to deescalate a potentially threatening situation.

The traits of courage, empathy, compassion, love, forgiveness, respect, are all character traits and concepts that can be learned, encouraged and demonstrated in professional practice. Nurse educators need to demonstrate the ability to call on these traits and behaviors to adequately respond to all of the collaborative interactions they find themselves in with colleagues, students, patients, community and family. When nurse faculty exhibit wisdom aka self-transcendence in all of our daily interactions the possibility for incivility to occur is reduced dramatically. This seminar is ultimately intended to assist nurse faculty to cultivate an attitude of grace under pressure which they can share with others by demonstration.

SECTION VI

CONCLUSION

Implications for nurse educators and nursing education include what Watson refers to as a bringing back of face to really see the people in front of us. It is possible for nurse educators to synthesize and engage the diversity of the sciences and humanities and to include notions of personal growth and transformational learning (Watson, 2008).

Watson (2008) further states that:

> Caritas educators of nurses and health care professionals thus face a double challenge in establishing, promoting and maintaining human-to-human dialogue and caring relationships as the epicenter of the curriculum and teaching. As noted, this applies not only to an ethos of the practice of health care but also to an ethos that permeates the education of health care practitioners, hence the double challenge of a philosophy and science of caring for education. (p. 261)

This project proposal aligns overall with the next steps needed to address the problem of incivility in nursing education by beginning with ourselves. Taking a look at what we can do as individuals right now, right here on a daily basis, instance by instance. The production of the seminar proposed is feasible and timely. Implications of the predicted new findings; such as increased job satisfaction, reduced faculty turnover, reduced student attrition, increased patient safety are all significant positive outcomes and have the potential to positively impact the quality of nursing education profoundly.

REFERENCES

Altmiller, G. (2012). Student perceptions of incivility in nursing education: Implications for educators. *Nursing Education Perspectives, 33*(1), 15-20. doi:10.5480/1536-5026-33.1.15

American Association of Colleges of Nursing (AACN) (2015), Retrieved from http://www.aacn.nche.edu/media-relations/NrsgShortageFS.pdf

American Bar Association (ABA) (2015). Retrieved from http://www.americanbar.org/content/dam/aba/events/labor_law/2012/03/national_conference_on_equal_employment_opportunity_law/mw2012eeo_eisenberg2.authcheckdam.pdf

American Holistic Nurses Association (AHNA). (2015). Retrieved from http://www.ahna.org/About-Us/What-is-Holistic-Nursing

Anthony, M., & Yastik, J. (2011). Nursing students' experiences with incivility in clinical education. *Journal of Nursing Education, 50*(3), 140-144. doi:10.3928/01484834-20110131-04

Avant, K. C. & Walker, L.O. (2011). Strategies for theory construction in nursing (5th ed.). Upper Saddle River, NJ: Prentice Hall.

Brown, B. (2012). *Daring greatly: How the courage to be vulnerable transforms the way we live, love, parent, and lead.* New York, NY: Gotham Books.

Brown, C. (2014). Empathy: A concept analysis.

Clark, C. M. (2013). *Creating and Sustaining Civility in Nursing Education.* Indianapolis, IN: Sigma Theta Tau International.

Clark, C. M., Nguyen, D. T., & Barbosa-Leiker, C. (2014). Student perceptions of stress, coping, relationships, and academic civility: A longitudinal study. *Nurse Educator, 39*, 170-174. doi:10.1097/NNE.0000000000000049

Clark, C. M. (2013). National study on faculty-to-faculty incivility: Strategies to foster collegiality and civility. *Nurse Educator, 38*(3), 98-102. doi:10.1097/NNE.0b013e31828dc1b2

Clark, C. M., Olender, L., Kenski, D., & Cardoni, C. (2013). Exploring and addressing faculty-to-faculty incivility in nursing education: A national perspective and literature review, *Journal of Nursing Education, 52*, 211-218.

Davis, K. (2013). Incivility in Nursing Education. *ASBN Update, 17*(3), 16-17.

Dyer, W. (2015). All God's children. Retrieved from http://www.drwaynedyer.com/blog/tag/mother-teresa/

Gagnon, M., Gagnon, J., Desmartis, M., & Njoya, M. (2013). The impact of blended teaching on knowledge, satisfaction, and self-directed learning in nursing undergraduates: A randomized, controlled trial. *Nursing Education Perspectives, 34*, 377-382. doi:10.5480/10-459

Hall, N. R. S., Altman, F., & Blumenthal, S. J. (1996). *Mind-body interactions and disease and psychoneuroimmunological aspects of health and disease: Proceedings of a conference sponsored by the reunion task force of the National Institutes of Health.* Orlando, FL: Health Dateline Press.

Hawkins, K. (2015). Feeling disrespected: An exploration of the extant Literature. *Nursing Science Quarterly, 28*(1), 8-12. doi:10.1177/0894318414558612

Houston, J. (2012). *The wizard of us: Transformational lessons from Oz.* New York, NY: Atria Books.

Houston, J. (1982). *The possible human: A course in enhancing your physical, mental & creative abilities.* New York, NY: Jeremy P. Tarcher/Putman.

Institute of Medicine (IOM) (US) Committee on the Work Environment for Nurses and Patient Safety; Page A, editor. Keeping Patients Safe: Transforming the Work Environment of Nurses. Washington (DC): National Academies Press (US); 2004. 8, Implementation Considerations and Needed Research. Retrieved from http://www.ncbi.nlm.nih.gov/books/NBK216195/

Koestler, J., & Konopasek,L. (2013). Guidebook for clerkship directors. Chapter 5: Instructional methods and strategies. Small group teaching methods. Retrieved from http://familymed.uthscsa.edu/ACE/chapter5.htm#smallgroup

Laschinger, H. K., Wong, C., Regan, S., Young-Ritchie, C., & Bushell, P. (2013). Workplace incivility and new graduate nurses' mental health. *Journal of Nursing Administration, 43*, 415-421. doi:10.1097/NNA.0b013e31829d61c6

Lerner, H. (2004). Fear, anxiety and other uninvited guests. New York, NY: Harper Collins.

Luparell, S. (2011). Academic education incivility in nursing: The connection between academia and clinical settings. *Critical Care Nurse, 31*(2), 92-95. doi:10.4037/ccn2011171

McCarthy, V. L., & Bockweg, A. (2013). The role of transcendence in a holistic view of successful aging: A concept analysis and model of transcendence in maturation and aging. *Journal of Holistic Nursing, 31*(2), 84-92. doi:10.1177/0898010112463492

Montenery, S. M., Walker, M., Sorensen, E., Thompson, R., Kirklin, D., White, R., & Ross, C. (2013). Millennial generation student nurses' perceptions of the impact of multiple technologies on learning. *Nursing Education Perspectives, 34*, 405-409. doi:10.5480/10-451

Morin, K. (2010). Fostering civility and zestful partnerships: A cosmic connection (part one) Karen Morin, Susan Luparell, Cynthia Clark, Kathleen Heinrich. (2010). *Reflections on Nursing Leadership, 36*(3).

Park, A. Jones, N. (2012) Oakland massacre: Shooter kills seven at Christian nursing school, TIME. Retrieved from http://content.time.com/time/nation/article/0,8599,2110909,00.html

Roberts, S. J. (2015). Lateral violence in nursing: A review of the past three decades. *Nursing Science Quarterly, 28*(1), 36-41. doi:10.1177/0894318414558614

Robertson, J. E. (2012). Can't we all just get along? A primer on student incivility in nursing education. *Nursing Education Perspectives, 33*(1), 21-26. doi:10.5480/1536-5026-33.1.21

Rowles, C. J., (2012). Strategies that promote critical thinking and active learning. In Billings, D., & Halstead, J. A. (Eds.). *Teaching in nursing: A guide for faculty (4th ed.).* (p. 258-284). St. Louis, MO: Saunders Elsevier.

Ruiz, D. M. (2000). *The four agreements: Companion book.* SanRafael, CA: Amber-Allen.

Sulkowski, M. L. & Lazarus, P. J. (2011). Contemporary responses to violent attacks on college campuses, *Journal of School Violence, 10*, 338-354. doi:10.1080/15388220.2011.602601

Tolle, E. (2004). *The power of now: A guide to spiritual enlightenment.* Novato, CA: New World Library.

Walker, D. D., van Jaarsveld, D. D., & Skarlicki, D. P. (2014). Exploring the effects of individual customer incivility encounters on employee incivility: The moderating roles of entity incivility and negative affectivity, *Journal of Applied Psychology, 99*, 151-161. doi:10.1037/a0034350

Watson, J. (2008). Nursing: The philosophy and science of caring (Rev. Ed.). Boulder, CO: University Press of Colorado.

APPENDIX

APPENDIX A

NO TOLERANCE POLICY AND PLEDGE

"Insert the Name of Your School of Nursing Here." Considers workplace bullying unacceptable and will not tolerate it under any circumstances. This policy shall apply to all students and employees, regardless of his or her employee status (i.e. managerial vs. hourly, full-time vs. part-time, employee vs. independent contractor). Any student or employee found in violation of this policy will be disciplined, up to and including immediate dismissal from the program or immediate termination. Independent contractors found to be in violation of this policy may be subject to contract cancellation.

"Insert the Name of Your School of Nursing Here." Defines bullying as persistent, malicious, unwelcome, severe and pervasive mistreatment that harms, intimidates, offends, degrades or humiliates a student or employee, whether verbal, physical or otherwise, in the classroom or clinical site and at the place of work and/or in the course of employment.

"Insert the Name of Your School of Nursing Here." Promotes a healthy workplace culture where all students and employees are able to work in an environment free of bullying behavior.

"Insert the Name of Your School of Nursing Here." Encourages all students and employees to report any instance of bullying behavior. Any reports of this type will be treated seriously, investigated promptly and impartially.

"Insert the Name of Your School of Nursing Here." Further encourages all students and employees to formally report any concerns of assault, battery, or other bullying behavior of a criminal nature to the local Police Department.

"Insert the Name of Your School of Nursing Here." Requires any student or employee who witnesses any bullying, irrespective of reporting relationship, to immediately report this conduct to the Human Resources Director.

"Insert the Name of Your School of Nursing Here." Will protect students and employees who report bullying conduct from retaliation or reprisal.

"Insert the Name of Your School of Nursing Here." Considers the following types of behavior to constitute workplace bullying.

Please note, this list is not meant to be exhaustive and is only offered by way of example:

- Staring, glaring or other nonverbal demonstrations of hostility;
- Exclusion or social isolation;
- Excessive monitoring or micro-managing;
- Work-related harassment (work-overload, unrealistic deadlines, meaningless tasks);
- Being held to a different standard than the rest of an employee's work group;
- Consistent ignoring or interrupting of an employee in front of co-workers;
- Personal attacks (angry outbursts, excessive profanity, or name-calling);
- Encouragement of others to turn against the targeted employee;
- Sabotage of a co-worker's work product or undermining of an employee's work performance;
- Stalking;

I _____ (your name) have read **"Insert the Name of Your School Nursing Here"** Workplace Incivility/Bullying No Tolerance Policy

I understand my rights and responsibilities as a student/employee of **(Insert the Name of Your School of Nursing Here)** under this No Tolerance Policy.

Signature _____ Date _____

Contacted Ms. Eisenberg on 2/15/14 by email to request permission to adapt her model for nursing.

Permission Received 2/20/2015

Provided by and Adapted with permission from:

Give Me Your Lunch Money! Dealing With Bullies in Today's Workplace

Model Anti-Bullying Policy1

Sue Ellen Eisenberg, Esq.,

Sue Ellen Eisenberg & Associates, P.C.,

33 Bloomfield Hills Parkway, Suite 145

Bloomfield Hills, MI 48304

see@seelawpc.com

Permission

 Inbox x

Cynthia Brown <brown131@nsuok.edu>   Feb 15

to see

I would like to ask your permission to use the Model Document found online.

http://www.americanbar.org/content/dam/aba/events/labor_law/2012/03/ national_conference_on_equal_employment_opportunity_law/mw2012eeo_eisenberg2. authcheckdam.pdf

I would like to use it as a template for a No Tolerance for Incivility Pledge that would be used by nursing faculty to teach the importance of civil behavior and professional conduct expected between faculty to faculty, student to faculty and student to student interactions.

I would cite you as the original source or could use the words adapted from? However you would like to see the citation is fine, please let me know.

This product will be part of my capstone project. I'm working to complete my MSN in nursing education and would really appreciate using your material as a base to work from.

Thank you for considering my request,

Cindy Brown, BSN, RN
NSU

Sue Ellen Eisenberg <see@seelawpc. com>

to me

You have my permission. i would enjoy being able to review your "capstone" project.

Sue Ellen

Sue Ellen Eisenberg
SUE ELLEN EISENBERG & ASSOCIATES, P.C.
33 Bloomfield Hills Parkway, Suite 145
Bloomfield Hills, MI 48304
(248) 258-5050 phone
(248) 258-5055 fax
see@seelawpc.com e-mail
www.seelawpc.com

Cynthia Brown <brown131@nsuok.edu>   Feb 21

to Sue

Thank you so much for the permission. I will share my adaptation with you in advance of submitting it for faculty review. I also want to make sure that I properly cite your work. Will be glad to share the end products with you this Spring or Summer, I may have to extend my program to be sure of a quality project. Again, thanks so much.

Sincerely, Cindy Brown

APPENDIX B

SEMINAR CONTENT OUTLINE

Introduction

Do not worry you do not have to become a buddist monk to discover meditation, you will not be asked to change your personality to become some kind of weird smile robot and everything presented here somewhere in the depths of your soul you already know. Sometimes we all need little reminders of our potential to live fully, freely and to be truly In-Service to others. As Nurse Educators this is all about developing collegialtiy, recognition of the efforts of our brothers and sisters and believing in them even when we see them at their worst. The Divine is present in everyone (Dyer, 2015). When we are experiencing difficulty it is our chance to grow, nurse educators that treat each other and students with respect during challenging moments grow intellectually and spiritually and ultimately benefit from the person presenting the uncivil behavior.

Module 1

Mind-Body Interactions and Disease, Effects of Stress, Uncivil Behavior – What it Looks Like, What it Feels Like, Faculty to Student Examples, Student to Faculty Examples, Student to Student Examples, Phsycophisological Response of the Body to Incivility, PTSD, Potential for Violence.

Module 2

If It Is To Be It Is Up To Me, We Have All Experienced It, Complaining and Crying Does Not Help, Building Resiliency Helps, Brene Brown – Shame,

Vulnerability, Empathy our Best Friend-Brene Brown Empathy Short Video, Brene Brown's (20min) TED TALK Theodore Roosevelt:The Man in the Arena Speech (It is not the critic who counts; not the man who points out how the strong man stumbles, or where the doer of deeds could have done them better. The credit belongs to the man who is actually in the arena, whose face is marred by dust and sweat and blood; who strives valiantly; who errs, who comes short again and again, because there is no effort without error and shortcoming; but who does actually strive to do the deeds; who knows great enthusiasms, the great devotions; who spends himself in a worthy cause; who at the best knows in the end the triumph of high achievement, and who at the worst, if he fails, at least fails while daring greatly, so that his place shall never be with those cold and timid souls who neither know victory nor defeat. Theodore Roosevelt), What is Wholeheartedness, Lerners – Fear, Anxiety and Other Uninvited Guests, Embrace Your Stage Fright, You are Enough

Module 3

Houston's – The Possible Human, Mensch Exercise, Tolles – The Power of Now, Mindfulness, Knowing, Appropriate Responses to Stressful Interactions, Keeping Your Cool, Emotional Inteligence, Resisting the Kneejerk Reaction, Deciding How You Really Feel About a Situation, Be the Change You Want to See in the World - Ghandi

Module 4

Ruiz – The Four Agreements, Being Impeccable with Your Word, Don't Take Anything Personally, Don't Make Assumptions, Always Do Your Best, Reflective Meditation, Self-Care, Compassion Fatigue and Job Burnout Prevention, Promotion of Increased Job Satisfaction.

Module 5

Houston's – The Wizard of Us, Brains, Courage, Heart, There's No Place Like Home, Nursing the Noble Profession, When Your Heart Get's Big, Learning through Adversity, Celebrating our Accomplishments

Module 6

Now What? Positive Attributes to Emphasize, Negative Behaviors to Stop, More on Self Care, Comittment and Recomittment to Your Daily Practice, Brene Brown: Listening to Shame video, Love and Forgiveness, Believe

Module 7

Taking it to the Classroom, Engaging Your Students, Colleagues and Community, Clinical Site Considerations, Reducing Nursing Student Stress Increases Patient Safety in the Clinical Environment, Other Resources and Suggested Reading for Nurse Educators

APPENDIX C

INSTITUTE OF MEDICINE RESEARCH ON COLLABORATIVE MODELS OF CARE

Chapter 5 and Appendix B review the benefits to patient safety that is likely to accrue as a result of effective inter-professional collaboration, including approaches to team care. Based on the evidence presented in Appendix B; the committee concludes that there is a need to better understand the mechanisms that produce effective collaboration and team processes:

- What interpersonal and group interaction processes contribute to effective collaboration and delivery of safe care? A number of theories exist concerning how teams perform and how their behaviors contribute to safe or unsafe practices. Additional information is needed about which of these theories are most applicable to the delivery of quality health care and which approaches in health care and other industries demonstrate the most potential for favorable effect.

- How can effective collaboration among groups of health care practitioners with differing characteristics—such as different skill levels (novice nurses versus competent, proficient, or expert nurses) and different duration of employment (e.g., rotating residents and float nurses)—be achieved? What other factors influence effective collaboration, and what strategies are effective in addressing them?

- How do environmental influences affect team performance? For example, what are the effects of stress, organizational culture, and leadership in facilitating or structuring collaborative care?

- How applicable are crew resource management principles and other non–health-related strategies in achieving collaboration and error reduction?

- How can more-productive interpersonal interactions be fostered across the multiple ways in which health care workers interact (e.g., in dyads, small groups, and unit-based teams)? What interpersonal behaviors facilitate effective interaction, decision making, and error prevention? How can these behaviors best be taught?

(IOM, 2004)

APPENDIX D

DISASTER PLAN

Each institution will need to adopt a disaster preparedness plan that may include threat assessment approaches. Unfortunately there is a tendency to underreport threatening individuals; which limits the opportunity for action by professionals who with access to important information may be able to prevent an attack (Sulkowski & Lazarus (2012). The importance of facilitating student faculty connectedness, campus climate, and respect for culturally diverse members of the campus cannot be overstressed (Sulkowski & Lazarus (2012).

APPENDIX E

NEEDS ASSESSMENT

1) Describe your faculty practice area.
   a) Adjunct Faculty
   b) Clinical Instructor
   c) LPN Program
   d) ADN Program
   e) Assistant Professor
   f) Professor
   g) Director/Administrator
2) Have you experienced incivility during your career?
   a) Yes
   b) No
   c) Unsure
3) Are you interested in cultivating techniques, attributes and skills to promote civility within your department, institution and community?
   a) Yes
   b) No
   c) Unsure
4) Describe your experiences pertaining to incivility in nursing education.
5) What types of teaching/learning opportunities would you be interested in surrounding the topic of incivility in nursing education?
   a) Online Seminars/Webinars
   b) Live Seminars
   c) CEU's
   d) Journal Articles
   e) None, not interested in the topic of incivility in nursing education.

APPENDIX F

POST-SEMINAR SURVEY

1) I am better equipped to deal with incivility constructively after having attended this seminar.
   a) Yes
   b) No
   c) Unsure
2) The concepts of empathy, compassion, forgiveness, love and courage are important to me; and I will use these new techniques to promote civility in my workplace.
   a) Yes
   b) No
   c) Unsure
3) I will re-energize my practice daily to include kindness and respect when working with colleagues, students and other clinicians during collaborative interactions.
   a) Yes
   b) No
   c) Unsure
4) I recognize the importance of adequately and appropriately coping with stressful situations as a mechanism to prevent incivility in my workplace and community settings.
   a) Yes
   b) No
   c) Unsure
5) What strategies will you employee to promote civility in your workplace and community settings?

6) I am concerned and want to prevent incivility in nursing education and plan to implement the tools to foster self-transcendence in my daily life, classroom and institution. I will (finish this sentence with actions you plan to take)............

APPENDIX G

FACILITATOR EVALUATION

1) The seminar was well organized.
   a) Strongly Agree
   b) Agree
   c) Neutral
   d) Disagree
   e) Strongly Disagree
2) The facilitator's teaching stimulated my interest in the subject.
   a) Strongly Agree
   b) Agree
   c) Neutral
   d) Strongly Disagree
3) The instructor treated students with respect.
   a) Strongly Agree
   b) Agree
   c) Neutral
   d) Disagree
   e) Strongly Disagree
4) The facilitator used teaching methods that helped understand the practical applications of the course content.
   a) Strongly Agree
   b) Agree
   c) Neutral
   d) Disagree
   e) Strongly Disagree

5) Relative to your knowledge at the beginning of this course, how would you rate the learning which you have achieved in the subject?
   a) Outstanding
   b) Very Good
   c) Good
   d) Adequate
   e) Poor
6) What aspects of the course contributed the least to your learning?
7) What recommendations do you have to improve the course?

TEACHING PLAN

OBJECTIVE	CONTENT
By the end of the seminar nursing faculty will: 1. Recognize incivility in nursing education. **Instructional Strategies:** Storytelling and Instructional 20 Minutes **Assessment Strategies:** Application: Demonstrate, Explain, Make Use of Knowledge **Instructional Strategies:** Instructional 5 Minutes	*Objective One:* Uncivil Behavior **What it Looks Like** Eye-Rolling, Gossiping, Raised Voices, Rude Behavior, Physical Violence Against a Person or Property **What it Feels Like** Humiliating, Embarrassing, Sickening, Bad, Hurtful **Examples of Incivility in Nursing Education** Berating Insulting and Allowing Setting Up Undermining Sabotaging Power Playing Derailing and Disgracing Excluding Gossiping Degrading Refusing

	Not Doing
	Justifying
	Blaming and Accusing
	Taking Credit
	Distracting and Disrupting
	Module 1
2. Realize that self-responsibility for civil behavior is the best defense to incivility in nursing education.	*Objective Two:* **Self Responsibility** **"If it Is to Be it is Up to Me."** One individual at a time, starting with ourselves; nurse educators have the ability to promulgate a culture of civility among colleagues, with students in the classroom, at clinical partner sites and in the community.
Instructional Strategies: Instructional/Motivational 10 Minutes **Assessment Strategies:** Valuing: Draw Conclusions, Defend, and Make Decisions	This project suggests that nurse educators who cultivate mindfulness, knowing, authentic learning and engage students with dignity and respect can curb if not stop incivility from creeping into the learning environment. **Module 2**
3. Recognize mind-body interactions and disease, effects of stress and psychophysiological response of the body to incivility, PTSD and potential for violence.	*Objective Three:* **Psychophysiological Response of the Body to Incivility** Hall, Altman & Blumenthal, (1996, pg. 16) points out that one of the most significant and really unexpected findings that fostered this new

Instructional Strategies: Instructional Motivational/ Storytelling 20 Minutes **Assessment Strategies:** Synthesis: Draw Conclusions, Find Connections, Derive and Make Comparisons	field of PNI was that the immune system can respond to chemicals secreted by the central nervous system. Effects of Long Term Stress **Oikos Christian University: School of Nursing Shooting** In the case of the Oikos Christian University: School of Nursing shooting in Oakland in 2012; a former student targeted the school of nursing and a particular administrator. Seven were left dead after the rampage. This was the worst school shooting in U.S. history since the Virginia Tech shooting in 2007 (Park & Jones, 2012). **PTSD and Potential for Violence** Incivility has been defined many times over and can be described as a toxic environment where interactions between people are uncivil, rude, unsociable, ungracious, impolite, disrespectful, cruel, or even violent. Bullying has become a more common buzzword; however bullying and incivility differ (Roberts, 2015). Bullying consists of victimization whereas incivility is found at times to be a lateral form of violence. **Module 1**

4. Discuss resiliency and the role resiliency plays in decreasing stress, anxiety, insecurity. **Instructional Strategies:** Virtual Learning 30 Minutes **Assessment Strategies:** Synthesis: Draw Conclusions, Find Connections, Derive, and Make Comparisons **Instructional Strategies:** Instructional 10 Minutes **Assessment Strategies:** Analysis: Find Parts in a Whole, Connections, Discern, Criticize and Make Comparisons **Instructional Strategies:** Instructional 10 Minutes	***Objective Four:*** **Self-Responsibility** **Building Resiliency Helps** **https://youtu.be/CL2jcwBc0HY** **Lerner's - Fear, Anxiety and Other Uninvited Guests** According to Lerner, when it comes to anxiety in the workplace we must think in terms of the system. Anxiety is not just something that happens within an individual. Connectedness between individuals in the system is powerful, everyone reacts to how the other manages their anxiety. Anxiety with the system will move through the system at very high speeds and is contagious. Luckily calm can spread the same way and getting a grip on our ability to manage our own stress and anxiety and the reactions we have to stressful situations is important (Lerner, 2004). **Embrace Your Stage Fright** Lerner discusses how public speaking taught her to embrace her mistakes in a self-loving way and to overcome her most dreaded situations.

Assessment Strategies: Understanding: Formulate Knowledge in Own Words, Explain, Account For, Show Differences	A since of humor and a willingness to not be so hard on herself and others when stressful and high anxiety environments present themselves is a calm and balancing reaction. Lastly she points out that you do not have to become a social activist to create conditions of safety for others to show up and be real (Lerner, 2004).
Instructional Strategies: Virtual Learning 110 Minutes **Assessment Strategies:** Analysis: Find parts in a whole and connections discern, criticize, and make comparisons	**You are Enough** **https://youtu.be/cUuXDZERxrk** **Module 2**
5. Apply mindful awareness, patience, and empathy to a daily practice of promoting civility in nursing education. **Instructional Strategies:** Virtual Learning 3 Minutes **Assessment Strategies:** Application: Demonstrate, Explain, Make Use of Knowledge	*Objective Five:* **Empathy - Our Best Friend** **https://youtu.be/1Evwgu369Jw?list=** **PLmvK0QBfWqL2G5B2vRlK3kgRO6P** **47Mm1u** **Module 2** **Self-Awareness**

Instructional Strategies: Instructional 5 Minutes **Assessment Strategies:** Application: Demonstrate, Explain, Make Use of Knowledge	**What is Self-Awareness?** McCarthy & Bockweg (2013) look at self-transcendence as component or concept of successful aging from a holistic viewpoint. Maslow's Theory of Self-Transcendence is reviewed in great detail and linked back to the original theory of self-actualization. Examples are laid outlaid in relation to generativity, connectedness and meaning in life.
Instructional Strategies: Instructional 10 Minutes **Assessment Strategies:** Application: Demonstrate, Explain, Make Use of Knowledge	**What is Self-Transcendence** McCarthy & Bockweg point out that: Maslow's definition is extrapolated as the form of the verb transcend and the meaning is to rise above or move beyond time, culture, self, and others. Maslow identified other self-transcendence behaviors as moving beyond weakness, fears, and dependency; transcending the opinions or expectations of others, such as social conventions, family roles, or a focus on others to the exclusion of self: achieving a since of unity with oneself, others – especially the next generation – and a higher power; and possessing an awareness of a greater meaning in life. (McCarthy and Bockweg, 2013, p. 86)

Instructional Strategies:	**Houston's – The Possible Human**
Instructional	Handout - The Art of High Practice
15 Minutes	Yiddish Archetypes – The Nebbish and The Mensch
Assessment Strategies:	The Nebbish – The Artist of Low Practice
Application: Demonstrate, Explain, Make Use of Knowledge	The Mensch – The Human Possibility in All of Us
	The Art of the Mensch
	(Exercise)
	(from Jean Houston's – The Possible Human, p. 127)
	Time: 30 Minutes
	Handout - The Art of the Mensch
	Canon In D | Pachelbel's Canon
Instructional Strategies:	**Tolle's – The Power of Now**
Instructional	Tolle speaks to the importance of always saying Yes to the present moment. He teaches that to watch the mechanics of the moment and allowing the present moment to be will help us to step out of resistance patterns.
5 Minutes	
Assessment Strategies:	
Basic Knowledge: Define, Declare, Recognize	Tolle also states, "The present moment is sometimes unacceptable, unpleasant or awful (Tolle, 1999, p. 35"
	Module 3

Instructional Strategies: Instructional 5 Minutes **Assessment Strategies:** Basic Knowledge: Define, Declare, Recognize	**Self Love, Self Forgiveness and Believe** **Commitment and Recommitment to** **Your Daily Practice** Not once and done training, it is teaching a way of being, knowing and constantly reframing interactions, exchanges and collaborative efforts to increase respect, communication, collaboration and ultimately to reinforce civil behavior through repetition and the daily practice. **Module 6**
Instructional Strategies: Instructional 5 Minutes **Assessment Strategies:** Basic Knowledge: Define, Declare, Recognize	**Evidenced Based Practice** **Taking it to the Classroom** When faculty practices empathy, patience, kindness and self-control; potentially any negative or uncivil exchange can be avoided, diffused or resolved. Often times we have to learn to treat ourselves with the same loving kindness first to truly be able to demonstrate and offer it to others. **Module 7**
6. Demonstrate appropriate responses to stressful situations to diffuse potentially uncivil exchanges.	*Objective Six:* **Brene Brown**

Instructional Strategies: Virtual/Experiential 2 Minutes **Assessment Strategies:** Application: Demonstrate, Explain, Make Use of Knowledge	**TED TALK** **The Man in the Arena Speech** https://www.youtube.com/watch?v=tdN9-DN09vk
Instructional Strategies: Virtual/Experiential 1.50 Minutes **Assessment Strategies:** Synthesis: Draw Conclusions, Find Connections, Derive, and Make Comparisons	**What is Wholeheartedness?** https://youtu.be/DZR0-WFUfeE **Module 2**
7. Distinguish best practices, intrapersonal relationships; inventory appropriate behaviors that promote civility in nursing education. **Instructional Strategies:** Instructional 10 Minutes	*Objective Seven:* **Evidenced Based Practice** **Taking it to the Classroom** When faculty practices empathy, patience, kindness and self-control; potentially any negative or uncivil exchange can be avoided, diffused or resolved. Often times we have to learn to treat ourselves with the same loving kindness first to truly be able to demonstrate and offer it to others.

Assessment Strategies:	Engaging Your Students
Synthesis: Draw Conclusions, Find Connections, Derive, and Make Comparisons	Listen Care Give **Trust in Emergence** **Forgive** **Module 7**
8. Plan self-nurturance practices, self-care practices to combat fatigue, job burnout and promote patience and increase job satisfaction. **Instructional Strategies:** Instructional/ Storytelling 10 Minutes **Assessment Strategies:** Synthesis: Draw Conclusions, Find Connections, Derive, and Make Comparisons **Instructional Strategies:** Virtual/ Experiential 16 Minutes **Assessment Strategies:** Valuing: Draw Conclusions, Defend, and Make Decisions	***Objective Eight:*** Self Confidence **Jean Houston's – The Wizard of Us** Challenging situations that we face daily could be a matter of changing something that is no longer working for us, or confronting someone with a difficult conversation, or just trying to achieve a goal. Moving through fear and finding courage to overcome the difficult tasks can be a developed skill (Houston, 2012). Brains, Courage, Heart - There's No Place Like Home https://youtu.be/etM2L3ac3a8 **Module 5** **Sincerity, Generosity and Honesty**

Instructional Strategies: Instrucional 5 Minutes **Assessment Strategies:** Valuing: Draw Conclusions, Defend, and Make Decisions	**Ruiz – The Four Agreements** Don Miguel Ruiz is a New York Times best-selling author and physician and describes the Toltec wisdom or code of conduct that he teaches; the importance of integrity, not taking anything personally, being unassuming and always doing your best are the first actions that any individual can take to personal happiness and freedom (Ruiz, 2000).
Instructional Strategies: Virtual/ Experiential/ Active 15 Minutes **Assessment Strategies:** Valuing: Draw Conclusions, Defend, and Make Decisions	**Reflective Meditation** https://youtu.be/1sQ0DTF2tAM **Module 4** **Sincerity, Generosity and Honesty** **Self-Care** Faculty who are rigid, devoid of caring, that reach out to students without respect and demonstrate the adherence to oppressive pedagogies are where the tug of war begins (Robertson, 2012). Faculty will do well to take self-responsibility for learning new ways and revisiting old ways of doing things that are self-nurturing. **Module 4**

Instructional Strategies: Instructional 5 Minutes **Assessment Strategies:** Analysis: Find Parts in a Whole, Connections, Discern, Criticize, and Make Comparisons	**Compassion Fatigue and Job Burnout Prevention** Incivility in nursing education has been well documented (Clark, 2013), and furthermore incivility has no place in nursing education. Our society in general has grown to be a more hostile in institutions of higher learning (Walker, van Jaarsveld & Skarlicki, 2011). The advent of social media has made it very easy for people to bully, make rude comments and essentially harass people anonymously in the past
Instructional Strategies: Instructional 5 Minutes **Assessment Strategies:** Valuing: Draw Conclusions, Defend, and Make Decisions	**Increasing Job Satisfaction** Given the previous exploratory research there is much to be done to find ways to decrease incivility in nursing education; this is the first place to start on the level of the individual, self-responsibility coupled with meaningful communication and a conscious decision to be giving in our interactions with others.
9. Value the nursing profession, learning through adversity, celebrate accomplishments. **Instructional Strategies:** Instructional 10 Minutes	***Objective Nine:*** **Self Confidence** **Nursing the Noble Profession** When nurse faculty exhibit wisdom aka self-transcendence in all of our daily

Assessment Strategies: Valuing: Draw Conclusions, Defend, and Make Decisions Synthesis: Draw Conclusions, Find Connections, Derive and Make Comparisons **Instructional Strategies:** Instructional 5 Minutes **Assessment Strategies:** Valuing: Draw Conclusions, Defend, and Make Decisions Synthesis: Draw Conclusions, Find Connections, Derive and Make Comparisons	interactions the possibility for incivility to occur is reduced dramatically. This seminar is ultimately intended to assist nurse faculty to cultivate an attitude of grace under pressure which they can share with others by demonstration. **When Your Heart Gets Big Learning Through Adversity** Clark, Nguyen & Barbosa-Leiker conducted a three year longitudinal study using descriptive, repeated-measures, survey design to describe nursing students perceptions of coping with stress and faculty student and faculty relationships. The research lays out potential strategies to promote civility in nursing education. The students described that communication, flexibility and encouragement from faculty could reduce stress and provide increased coping abilities. These students also discussed activities that promoted stress reduction included talking with family and friends and spending time outdoors reduced their stress surrounding their academic pursuits.

Instructional Strategies: Instructional 5 Minutes **Assessment Strategies:** Valuing: Draw Conclusions, Defend, and Make Decisions Synthesis: Draw Conclusions, Find Connections, Derive and Make Comparisons	**Celebrating Our Accomplishments** Hawkins (2015) review reveals that the concepts of respect and disrespect reflect a rhythmical pattern and is often a perception denoted by communication. The way we communicate with people denotes to them whether or not we respect or disrespect them. Demonstrating value rather than conveying derogatory remarks communicates respect. Oppositely, disrespect was found in the literature to mostly coincide with the recipients feelings of anger, shame and uncertainty.
	Module 5
10. Select positive attributes to emphasize, negative behaviors to stop, implementation of these attributes and behaviors. **Instructional Strategies:** Instructional 5 Minutes **Assessment Strategies:** Application: Demonstrate, Explain, Make Use of Knowledge	*Objective Ten:* **Self-Love, Self-Forgiveness and Believe Now What?** Students are listening, watching; when they experience successful interactions they will mirror those behaviors and attitudes that they find to be pleasant. When students are shown a kindness especially when the specifics surrounding a particular interaction have the potential to be negative it can have the biggest impact.

Instructional Strategies:	Positive Attributes to Emphasize
Instructional	Good Nutrition
5 Minutes	Restful Sleep
	Self-Love
Assessment Strategies:	Faithfulness
Application: Demonstrate,	Uplifting Speech
Explain, Make Use of Knowledge	Positive Thoughts
Instructional Strategies:	**Negative Behaviors to Stop**
Instructional	Poor Nutrition
5 Minutes	Sleep Deprivation
	People Pleasing
Assessment Strategies:	Worrying
Application: Demonstrate,	Complaining
Explain, Make Use of Knowledge	Negative Thoughts
Instructional Strategies:	**More on Self Care**
Instructional	Me Time
2 Minutes	Exercise
	Stress Reducing Activities
Assessment Strategies: Valuing:	Family Time
Draw Conclusions, Defend, and	Being in Nature
Make Decisions	

11. Prepare to engage students, colleagues, clinical sites and community.	***Objective Eleven:*** **Evidenced Based Practice**
Instructional Strategies: Instructional 20 Minutes **Assessment Strategies:** Application: Demonstrate, Explain, Make Use of Knowledge	**Engaging Your Students** Listen Care Give Trust in Emergence Forgive **Colleagues and Community** **Clinical Site Considerations** People are naturally going to cooperate more fully when their feelings are considered and when they feel safe. A conscious decision to use non-threatening, supportive communication at all times and particularly in times of high stress, intense responsibility and also when differences of opinion need to be explored civilly is the place to start (Clark, 2013). **Reducing Nursing Student Stress Increases Patient Safety in the Clinical Environment** Researchers also stress the multiple ways in which health care workers interact in dyads, small groups, and unit-based teams, focusing on the characteristics of the interpersonal behaviors that facilitate effective interaction, decision making,

	and error-prevention performance may be more useful than a restricted focus on team behavior (IOM, 2004).
	Module 7
	No Tolerance Policy Template
12. Appraise and choose classroom tools such as the No Tolerance Incivility Policy and Pledge.	*Objective Twelve:*
	Handout- No Tolerance Policy Template
	Module 7
Instructional Strategies: Active/ Experiential	
5 Minutes	
Assessment Strategies:	
Analysis: Find Parts in a Whole, Connections, Discern, Criticize, and Make Comparisons	
Synthesis: Draw Conclusions, Find Connections, Derive and Make Comparisons	
Valuing: Draw Conclusions, Defend, and Make Decisions	

Printed in the United States
By Bookmasters